# Cursive Alphabet Practice for Left Handed

Name:_____

# Introduction

This no-frills book looks to help your student master their cursive handwriting skills! As you will recognize in this book, there aren't any distractions that will take up more time than the actual handwriting practice. THIS BOOK IS PRACTICE PRACTICE PRACTICE! With a little discipline and motivation, this book will not only help reinforce the student's strengths but also work on their weaknesses. That way, they spend less time on workbooks and more time enjoying other activities!

# Name:_____

Please trace over the letters and repeat into the remaining blanks.

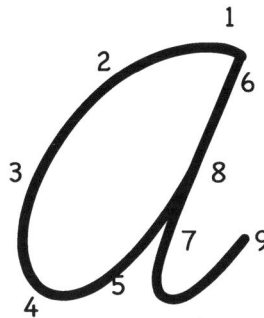

$a$

1
2
6
3
8
7
9
5
4

$a$ $a$ $a$ $a$ $a$

Name:_____

This page is intentionally left blank.

Name:_____

Please trace over the letters and repeat into the
remaining blanks.

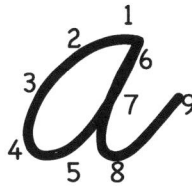

$a$
2 1
3   6
    7   9
4 5 8

$a$  $a$  $a$  $a$  $a$

Name:_____

This page is intentionally left blank.

Name:_____

Please trace over the letters and repeat into the
remaining blanks.

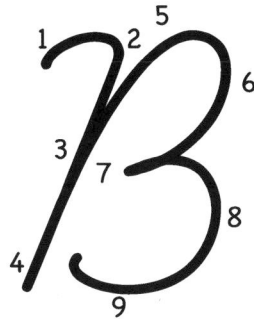

$\mathcal{B}$

$\mathcal{B}$ $\mathcal{B}$ $\mathcal{B}$ $\mathcal{B}$ $\mathcal{B}$

Name:_____

This page is intentionally left blank.

Name:_____

Please trace over the letters and repeat into the remaining blanks.

4   3
1   2   7
  8   9
5

b   b   b   b   b

Name:_____

This page is intentionally left blank.

Please trace over the letters and repeat into the remaining blanks.

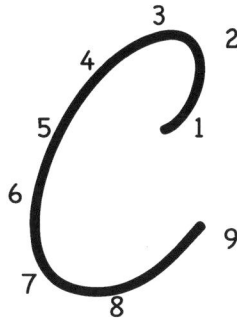

$C$ $C$ $C$ $C$ $C$

Name:_____

This page is intentionally left blank.

Please trace over the letters and repeat into the remaining blanks.

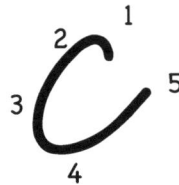

$C$

1
2
3
5
4

$C$  $C$  $C$  $C$  $C$

Name:_____

This page is intentionally left blank.

Name:_____

Please trace over the letters and repeat into the
remaining blanks.

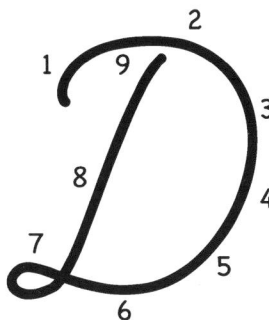

$\mathcal{D}$ $\mathcal{D}$ $\mathcal{D}$ $\mathcal{D}$ $\mathcal{D}$

Name:_____

This page is intentionally left blank.

# Name:_____

Please trace over the letters and repeat into the remaining blanks.

d

6
1  5
2
4
8
3    7

d  d  d  d  d

Name:_____

This page is intentionally left blank.

# Name:_____

Please trace over the letters and repeat into the remaining blanks.

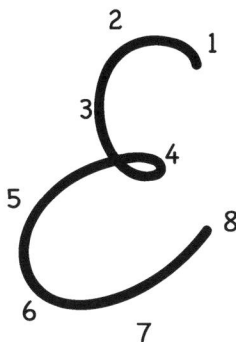

$\mathcal{E}$

$\mathcal{E}$ $\mathcal{E}$ $\mathcal{E}$ $\mathcal{E}$ $\mathcal{E}$ — — — — — — — — — — —

— — — — — — — — — — — — — — — — — — — — — —

— — — — — — — — — — — — — — — — — — — — — —

Name:_____

This page is intentionally left blank.

Name:_____

Please trace over the letters and repeat into the
remaining blanks.

$e$

3  2
4  1  6
5

*e  e  e  e  e*

Name:_____

This page is intentionally left blank.

Name:_____

Please trace over the letters and repeat into the remaining blanks.

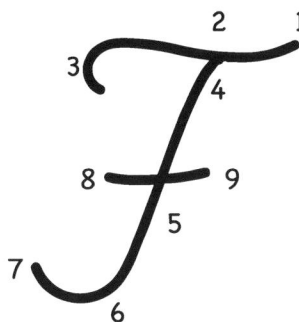

2  1
3 $\mathcal{F}$ 4
8    9
5
7
6

$\mathcal{F}$ $\mathcal{F}$ $\mathcal{F}$ $\mathcal{F}$ $\mathcal{F}$ – – – – – – – – – –

– – – – – – – – – – – – – – – – – – – –

– – – – – – – – – – – – – – – – – – – –

Name:_____

This page is intentionally left blank.

# Name:_____

Please trace over the letters and repeat into the
remaining blanks.

$f$ $f$ $f$ $f$ $f$

Name:_____

This page is intentionally left blank.

Name:_____

Please trace over the letters and repeat into the remaining blanks.

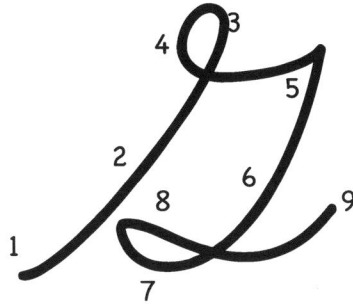

Name:_____

This page is intentionally left blank.

# Name:_____

Please trace over the letters and repeat into the
remaining blanks.

2 $g$ 1 5

4

3 9

8 6

7

$g$ $g$ $g$ $g$ $g$

Name:_____

This page is intentionally left blank.

Name:_____

Please trace over the letters and repeat into the remaining blanks.

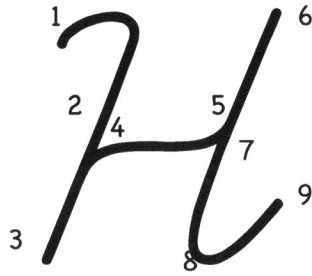

$\mathcal{H}$  $\mathcal{H}$  $\mathcal{H}$  $\mathcal{H}$  $\mathcal{H}$

Name:_____

This page is intentionally left blank.

# Name:_____

Please trace over the letters and repeat into the remaining blanks.

$h$

3
4
5  2
1  8
  7  9
6

$h$  $h$  $h$  $h$  $h$

Name:_____

This page is intentionally left blank.

# Name:_____

Please trace over the letters and repeat into the remaining blanks.

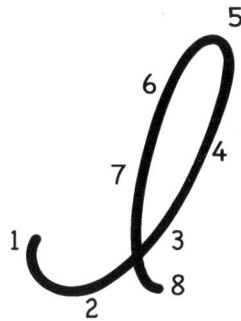

$l$ $l$ $l$ $l$ $l$

Name:_____

This page is intentionally left blank.

Name:_____

Please trace over the letters and repeat into the remaining blanks.

$i$

_i_  _i_  _i_  _i_  _i_

Name:_____

This page is intentionally left blank.

Name:_____

Please trace over the letters and repeat into the
remaining blanks.

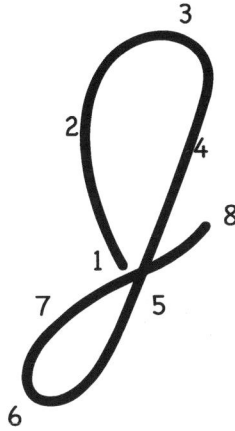

$J$

$\mathcal{J}$ $\mathcal{J}$ $\mathcal{J}$ $\mathcal{J}$ $\mathcal{J}$

Name:_____

This page is intentionally left blank.

Please trace over the letters and repeat into the remaining blanks.

*j   j   j   j   j*

Name:_____

This page is intentionally left blank.

Please trace over the letters and repeat into the remaining blanks.

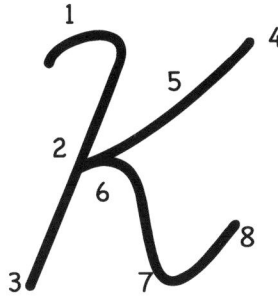

$\mathcal{K}$ 
1
2
3
4
5
6
7
8

$\mathcal{K}$ $\mathcal{K}$ $\mathcal{K}$ $\mathcal{K}$ $\mathcal{K}$

Name:_____

This page is intentionally left blank.

Name:_____

Please trace over the letters and repeat into the remaining blanks.

$k$ $k$ $k$ $k$ $k$

Name:_____

This page is intentionally left blank.

Name:_____

Please trace over the letters and repeat into the remaining blanks.

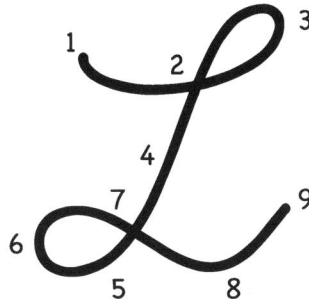

$L$  $L$  $L$  $L$  $L$

Name:_____

This page is intentionally left blank.

# Name:_____

Please trace over the letters and repeat into the remaining blanks.

$\ell$

1 2 3 4 5 6 7

$\ell$ $\ell$ $\ell$ $\ell$ $\ell$

Name:_____

This page is intentionally left blank.

Name:_____

Please trace over the letters and repeat into the remaining blanks.

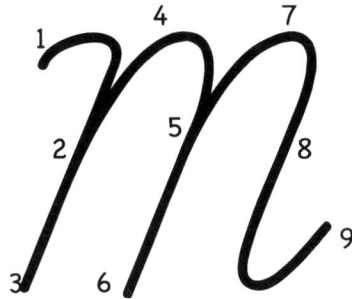

$m$

$m$ $m$ $m$ $m$ $m$

Name:_____

This page is intentionally left blank.

Please trace over the letters and repeat into the remaining blanks.

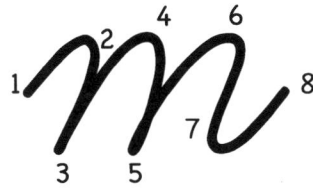

1 2 4 6 8
m
3 5 7

m    m    m    m    m

Name:_____

This page is intentionally left blank.

Name:_____

Please trace over the letters and repeat into the remaining blanks.

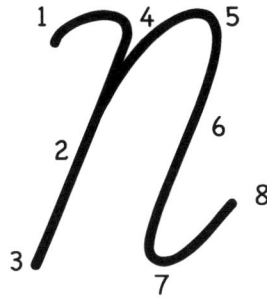

n n n n n

Name:_____

This page is intentionally left blank.

Name:_____

Please trace over the letters and repeat into the remaining blanks.

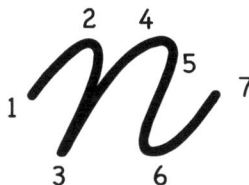

$n$

2  4
1   $n$  5  7
3     6

$n$    $n$    $n$    $n$    $n$

Name:_____

This page is intentionally left blank.

Name:_____

Please trace over the letters and repeat into the remaining blanks.

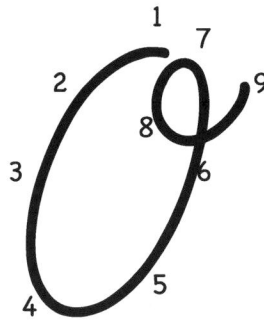

$\mathcal{O}$ $\mathcal{O}$ $\mathcal{O}$ $\mathcal{O}$ $\mathcal{O}$ — — — — — — — — — — —

Name:_____

This page is intentionally left blank.

Please trace over the letters and repeat into the
remaining blanks.

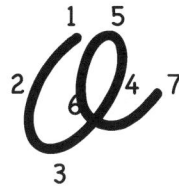

1  5
2     4  7
    6
3

𝒶  𝒶  𝒶  𝒶  𝒶

Name:_____

This page is intentionally left blank.

Name:_____

Please trace over the letters and repeat into the remaining blanks.

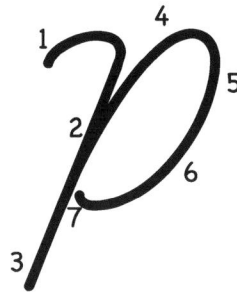

$p$ $p$ $p$ $p$ $p$ - - - - - - - - - - - - - - -

- - - - - - - - - - - - - - - - - - - - - -

- - - - - - - - - - - - - - - - - - - - - -

Name:_____

This page is intentionally left blank.

Name:_____

Please trace over the letters and repeat into the remaining blanks.

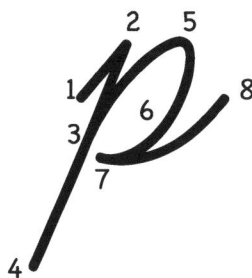

2   5
1  $p$
3   6   8
7
4

$p$  $p$  $p$  $p$  $p$

Name:_____

This page is intentionally left blank.

Please trace over the letters and repeat into the remaining blanks.

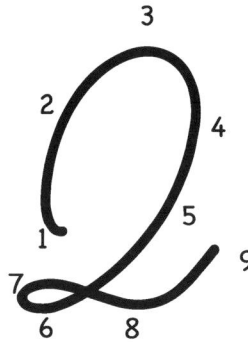

*Q 2 2 2 2*

Name:_____

This page is intentionally left blank.

Name:_____

Please trace over the letters and repeat into the remaining blanks.

q

1
2
5
4
9
3 6
8
7

q q q q q

Name:_____

This page is intentionally left blank.

Name:_____

Please trace over the letters and repeat into the
remaining blanks.

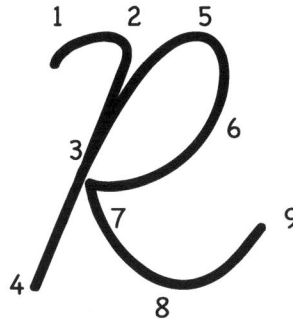

1  2  5
3  6
7  9
4  8

R  R  R  R  R

Name:_____

This page is intentionally left blank.

Please trace over the letters and repeat into the remaining blanks.

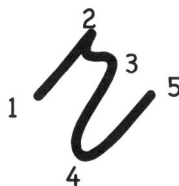

Name:_____

This page is intentionally left blank.

Please trace over the letters and repeat into the
remaining blanks.

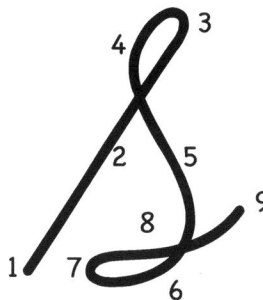

Name:_____

This page is intentionally left blank.

# Name:_____

Please trace over the letters and repeat into the remaining blanks.

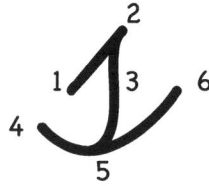

$J$ $J$ $J$ $J$ $J$

Name:_____

This page is intentionally left blank.

# Name:_____

Please trace over the letters and repeat into the remaining blanks.

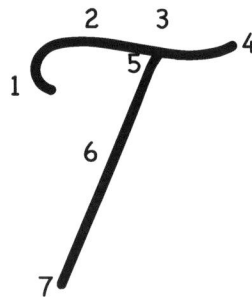

$T$

2  3
1  5  4
6
7

$\mathcal{F}$ $\mathcal{F}$ $\mathcal{F}$ $\mathcal{F}$ $\mathcal{F}$

Name:_____

This page is intentionally left blank.

# Name:_____

Please trace over the letters and repeat into the remaining blanks.

$t$

$t$ $t$ $t$ $t$ $t$

Name:_____

This page is intentionally left blank.

Name:_____

Please trace over the letters and repeat into the remaining blanks.

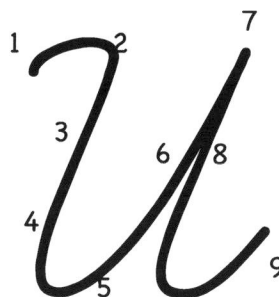

$\mathcal{U}$

1  2  7
3
4  6  8
5  9

$\mathcal{U}$  $\mathcal{U}$  $\mathcal{U}$  $\mathcal{U}$  $\mathcal{U}$

Name:_____

This page is intentionally left blank.

Please trace over the letters and repeat into the remaining blanks.

2  5
1  4  7
3
6

$\mathcal{U}$  $\mathcal{U}$  $\mathcal{U}$  $\mathcal{U}$  $\mathcal{U}$

Name:_____

This page is intentionally left blank.

Name:_____

Please trace over the letters and repeat into the remaining blanks.

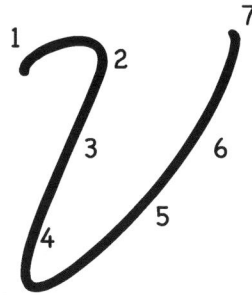

$\mathcal{V}$

1  2  7
  3   6
 4   5

$\mathcal{V}$ $\mathcal{V}$ $\mathcal{V}$ $\mathcal{V}$ $\mathcal{V}$ _ _ _ _ _ _ _ _ _ _ _ _

Name:_____

This page is intentionally left blank.

Name:_____

Please trace over the letters and repeat into the
remaining blanks.

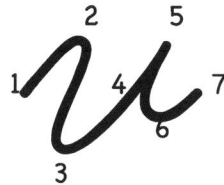

2   5
1   4   7
3

_u_   _u_   _u_   _u_   _u_

Name:_____

This page is intentionally left blank.

Name:_____

Please trace over the letters and repeat into the
remaining blanks.

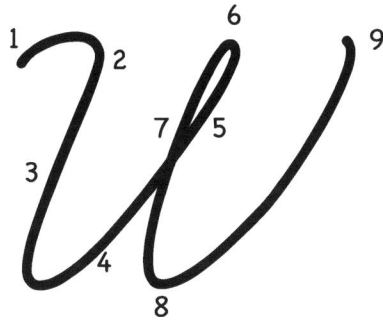

$\mathcal{W}$ $\mathcal{W}$ $\mathcal{W}$ $\mathcal{W}$ $\mathcal{W}$

Name:_____

This page is intentionally left blank.

# Name:_____

Please trace over the letters and repeat into the remaining blanks.

$w$

1 2 4 6 8 3 5 7

$w$ $w$ $w$ $w$ $w$

Name:_____

This page is intentionally left blank.

Name:_____

Please trace over the letters and repeat into the
remaining blanks.

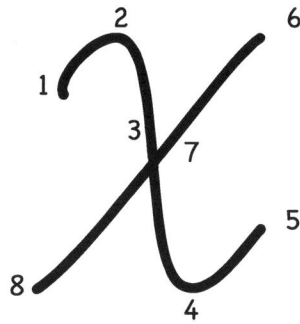

$\chi$ $\chi$ $\chi$ $\chi$ $\chi$

Name:_____

This page is intentionally left blank.

Please trace over the letters and repeat into the
remaining blanks.

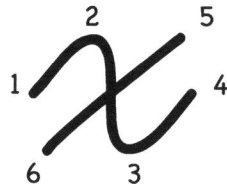

2   5
1   $x$   4
6   3

$x$   $x$   $x$   $x$   $x$

Name:_____

This page is intentionally left blank.

# Name:_____

Please trace over the letters and repeat into the remaining blanks.

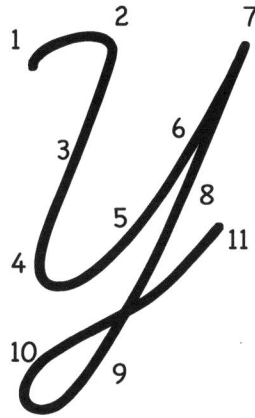

$\mathcal{Y}$  $\mathcal{Y}$  $\mathcal{Y}$  $\mathcal{Y}$  $\mathcal{Y}$

Name:_____

This page is intentionally left blank.

Please trace over the letters and repeat into the remaining blanks.

$y$

2   4
1   8
3   5
7
6

$y$   $y$   $y$   $y$   $y$

Name:_____

This page is intentionally left blank.

Name:_____

Please trace over the letters and repeat into the
remaining blanks.

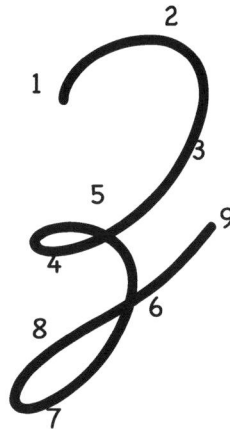

$3$ $3$ $3$ $3$ $3$

Name:_____

This page is intentionally left blank.

Name:_____

Please trace over the letters and repeat into the remaining blanks.

*z*  $\begin{smallmatrix}1 & & 2 \\ & & \\ 3 & & 7 \\ 6 & 4 \\ 5 & \end{smallmatrix}$

*z   z   z   z   z*

Name:_____

This page is intentionally left blank.

**Name:**_____

Please trace over the curisve letters. Then, please copy the cursive letters into the space provided.

*A B C D E F G H I J K*

*L M N O P Q R S T U V*

*W X Y Z* - - - - - - - - - - - - - - - -

*a b c d e f g h i j k l m n o p q r s t u v w x y z*

Name:_____

This page is intentionally left blank.

**Name:**_____

*A B C D E F G H I J K*

*L M N O P Q R S T U V*

*W X Y Z*

*a b c d e f g h i j k l m n o p q r s t u v w x y z*

Name:_____

End

Printed in Great Britain
by Amazon